TIME MANAGEMENT

LESSONS FROM 10 SUCCESSFUL AND WEALTHY PEOPLE ABOUT TIME MANAGEMENT AND PRODUCTIVITY.

By

PAUL GOLEMAN

TABLE OF CONTENTS

INTRODUCTION

Improvement is a gradual process. If you are not productive today, you will be one day if you continue to work on it and practice productivity hacks consistently. You will fail so many times, and there will times when you feel like giving up, but remember, people succeed only when they learn to get over the setbacks and start all over. There will be other individuals who will likewise read this book. They will also learn productivity improvement strategies and tool. They will outperform you if they manage to continue their improvement journey and make consistent efforts.

So this book is your first stepping stone. This book will give you a direction about productivity improvement tools and methodologies. You will know how successful people thrive on their strengths and live their dream. But in the end, you will have to take action to implement those exercises in your day to day life. I wish you luck. Hope you find your life purpose and make the universe work in your favor. Let's get started!

CHAPTER 1: HOW TO BE NOTORIOUSLY PRODUCTIVE TO BE INSANELY SUCCESSFUL?

CAN YOU MASTER RICHARD BRANSON'S PRODUCTIVITY EXERCISES?

Life is pretty simple. Do not make it hard and unnecessarily complicated. You will be better at time management if you can effectively organize your time to meet your priorities. So what comes first? Before anything, it is important that you set your daily goals and priorities.

Yes, you have to know what tasks are most important to you today. Then organize your time in a way so that you can address them without having to kill yourself. Business magnet, Richard Branson, believes that everyone can do it. One of his most important advices is that you should learn punctuality. This means that you should always try to be on time. Here is what Sir Richard Branson has to say about productivity;

"If you want to be more productive, then start at the start: get there on time,"
(https://www.linkedin.com/pulse/productivity-hacks-want-more-productive-punctual-richard-branson?trk=prod-inf-productivityhacks-1015-amyspost)

Being punctual does not mean that you have to complete all your tasks or make room for everything in your schedule. No, it is not important that you have to rush around all the time. Being punctual means that you have to be efficient in organizing your time. So how do you start?

STEP 1 # TRY

Richard Branson believes trying is the ideal thing you should do to begin. You do not have to be perfect at time organization. You do not have to punish yourself if you cannot be on time all the time. But, it takes nothing to try. The point is that you have to try to be punctual. That way you at least take repeated actions to make yourself disciplined, focused, and organized. Set your intentions right. If you want to ensure that you are able to complete at least 80 percent of your tasks today, you have to try to complete 100 percent.

STEP 2 # LEARN HOW TO STOP WASTING TIME

The primary intention of trying to be punctual is to stop wasting time. You can be more productive if you can use your time effectively. For example, if you have to attend a meeting, you try hard to be at the assembly point right on time. But, despite all your efforts, if you find out that you cannot be there or attend the meeting no matter how hard you try, intimate others about your status and apologize. The time you set aside for that meeting earlier can be reassigned for the next important task. This is how you use your time.

STEP 3 # MAKE IT A HABIT

Try to be punctual and make it a habit. It is not going to happen initially. But as you try again and again, you will master the skill gradually. After a certain point in time, you will feel being punctual is effortlessly easy. So do not be too hard on yourself. Give yourself time to develop the habit.

In addition, Richard Branson also believes that your productivity depends on how you inspire yourself. Embrace the elements of joy for inspiration. This is empowering. Do what makes you feel motivated during the toughest times. If you follow your passion, time management will be easy. You will feel the drive to keep up the efforts during the challenging moments. Make every minute of your life useful.

CHAPTER 2: YOUR SUCCESS WILL BE EMPOWERED WITH THIS POWERFUL HABIT

READ WHAT MARK ZUCKERBERG DOES TO BE PRODUCTIVE

To help your mind focus better and complete a task time efficiently, you must give it some treat frequently. Your brain also needs to unplug and refresh from time to time. Facebook founder, Mark Zuckerberg, also feels the same way.

Believe it or not, your habit is one of the crucial determinants of your success. How do you think, how do you manage your time, how do you relax and boost your mental health, how do you concentrate on your work; these all matter a lot for efficient time management and getting important work done. What can you do to give your brain some time off and relax for a moment?

Mark Zuckerberg announced earlier that reading habit is going to be one of his priorities in 2015. He decided to become a voracious reader. That makes sense because reading habit is scientifically proven to be very helpful for brain and mental health.

Besides the well-known fact that reading books is a powerful knowledge building habit, it is also beneficial for reducing stress; building a creative mind; improving memory, thinking skill, focus, and attention. Many amazing things happen when you develop a reading habit. We all know our mental and brain health contribute significantly to our productivity overall.

So here are few amazing benefits that come along this wonderful habit:

1. Reading habit is good for mental stimulation: http://www.lifehack.org/articles/lifestyle/10-benefits-reading-why-you-should-read-everyday.html. It keeps the brain active and helps to slow down the process of brain aging. Any kind of activity which engages the brain muscles can help you protect your brain's cognitive functions like memory and thinking ability. So reading can be one of the most powerful ways to improve the brain's functions.

2. Read to de-stress: After a lot of stressful work, if you wish to unplug for a moment so that you can concentrate better, then reading a book can be the best way to do that. For maximum productivity, you need to keep the impact of stress as low as possible. Reading a nice inspiring book can immediately divert your mind from the troubles and help you get your enthusiasm back. This will help you focus better and complete tasks faster.

3. Reading a book can be a very helpful habit for improving focus and concentration: When you read, you only concentrate on that specific task that is reading. You do not attempt to multitask. That's because when you read, you cannot check your emails, attend a conference call, etc., simultaneously. This is why this habit helps you to build a strong focus and attention skill.

Reading is also a free entertainment source. You can read different types of books to elevate your mood and forget the worries and problems for some time. It helps people to get over anxiety and refocus. This is why reading habit can be a powerful productivity hack.

Next, you will learn how Oprah Winfrey challenges stress with her routine schedule and gets what she wants.

CHAPTER 3: USE YOUR TIME BEFORE YOU LOSE IT

LEARN PRODUCTIVITY OPRAH WINFREY'S WAY

There is no magic formula. How you manage your time and day simply depends on your habits. And habits can be changed. Oprah Winfrey is a globally recognized name. However, she was not this famous initially. She had many struggles like any ordinary man. But, she survived all traumatic life circumstances as she found out ways to get stronger and work on her dreams.

Oprah Winfrey has her own ways to deal with intense life problems. She believes that key to her overwhelming success is her radical focus. She manages her stress efficiently so that she can focus on her goals uninterruptedly. Here are a few things she does to keep her stress away and live her days more productively:

1. She Never Gives Up Her Sleep For Work: We all know how important sleep is to allow the brain function well. Oprah Winfrey strictly follows her sleep schedule to maintain her focus. She sleeps at least for five and a half an hour every day as she cannot focus and concentrate if she sleeps less than that. Brain's cognitive functions decline sharply due to lack of sleep for a very long time. So try not to ignore sleep if you want to improve your productivity.

2. Her Morning Routine: You can develop few specific morning habits to make your brain sharp and focused. For example, Oprah Winfrey practices mindfulness to keep her mind and consciousness active. Mindfulness is the practice of improving awareness. So, that way she becomes more focused at her work. It can be a nice idea for anyone who struggles to concentrate on work.

3. Her Tricks to Avoid Procrastinations: Procrastination can be a huge deal if it becomes a dominating habit. You will continue to avoid important tasks and your backlog will increase. Many people fail to change this habit and this is why stress and tensions continue to increase in their life. Oprah Winfrey is a huge procrastinator too. She takes time to get over uncomfortable conversations and confrontal things. But her strategy to beat procrastination is thinking about the worst. When she attempts to procrastinate to get rid of some uncomfortable situations, she tries to imagine the worst. It helps her stop delaying her work if she knows she can survive the worst.

4. She Reads Motivational Quotes: You have to find out your ways to be more productive. For example, Oprah Winfrey discovered she gets extra inspiration boost when she reads motivational quotes. So, after waking up in the morning when she waits for her tea to brew and stands in the kitchen, she quickly read few motivational quotes from different experts. Starting the day with an optimistic mindset is an amazing idea.

You can do that when you feel lost and think you need some direction.

Life is full of inspirational opportunities for improvements. You just have to identify them and adapt. Productivity improves as soon as your lifestyle and habits improve. You will have to be aware of your habits, weaknesses, and the struggles that always hold you back. Then work hard to understand and strengthen your strengths so that you can beat the bad habits away and live a more productive and successful life.

What comes next? Next, you will read Warren Buffet's productivity strategy. He is an amazing entrepreneur who knows how to make life simple and successful. Let's read.

CHAPTER 4: WHERE DO YOU MAKE MISTAKES?

FOLLOW WARREN BUFFET'S 2 LIST STRATEGY TO GET MORE WORK DONE

Who does not know Warren Buffet? Who would not like to be like him? He is a super busy man who always is buried under the never ending work burden. But, he is managing his work, building empires, and earning money consistently. How does he manage his days? He is not a mutant, is he? He has no super powers. But, he does something different which gives him an advantage over cutthroat competitions. So how does Warren Buffet maximize his productivity and get more work done?

Warren Buffet lives his life by two simple rules. This is how he plans his days and work:

RULE 1 # NARROW DOWN PRIORITIES

He only and only works on 5 priorities every day. This means that you might have several work goals for a day, but you should narrow them down to 5 most essential work goals that you must work on no matter what.

A short story came in the media a year back: According to sources, once, Warren Buffet and his personal airplane pilot, Mike Flint, was having a conversation on career strategies. Mike Flint was discussing career priorities with Warren Buffet during the conversation. Warren Buffet told Flint to write down 25 career goals, so he did; Flint wrote the 25 career goals and showed it to Buffet.

Then Buffet told Flint to circle 5 goals that he thinks is most crucial for him. Flint took a bit time to understand his priorities and then circled 5 goals he thought was most important for him. When Buffet asked him what he was going to do with the remaining 20 goals that he did not circle, Flint replied that he would work on them intermittently as they were not his priorities.

Warren Buffet then corrected him, saying that those 20 goals that he did not circle needed to be eliminated entirely. Hence, the second rule:

RULE 2 # ELIMINATE WHAT IS NOT NECESSARY

Buffet believes one of the best ways to make life simple and successful is to eliminate that which is unnecessary so that you can focus only on what is important. Warren Buffet is a believer of minimalism. He thinks that minimalism helps him to reduce distractions and stay focused and productive. This makes sense.

You will be crazy if you attempt to do everything on your own. You cannot do that without any superhuman powers. You will soon lose interest at work, feel overwhelmed and give up. You have to learn to narrow down your daily goals and focus on a few handful of things that you think you must work on. Forget about those that are not important; you do not need to work on the rest. More accurately, if you prioritize and eliminate, the better you are at productivity.

So this is how Warren Buffet stands out. Think you can do that? Try them out.

Next, you will know some amazing habits of Jeff Bezos. He is a master stress reliever. He knows how to keep his mind stress free. Let's find out his methods and strategies to be more productive.

CHAPTER 5: SIMPLE TRICK TO BE MORE PRODUCTIVE

HOW JEFF BEZOS MAKES HIS MIND STRESS FREE

Well, you will be surprised to know how creative entrepreneurs can be in managing theirs hours of sleep. Jeff Bezos is one of those entrepreneurs who know that without enough sleep, clarity of thoughts does not come. So here are his advises:

1. Never Cut Back on Your Sleep

Do you want productivity? Well, you cannot have that if you continue to ignore your sleep hours. This is what Jeff Bezos believes personally. If you are working hard on your personal and professional goals, then you need to have enough hours of sleep to restore your physical and brain power.

Amazon.com founder Jeff Bezos needs eight of hours of sleep every day to keep up with his daily challenges. Instead of overworking, he believes in work prioritization and addressing few key concerns daily. That way he can complete all his important tasks without being sleep deprived.

If you are not able to focus on your work or feel like that you do not have mental clarity, long-term sleep deprivation can be one of the reasons. It is very important that you closely observe your day to day schedule. How long have you been ignoring sleep? Again, the amount of sleep required might differ from person to person. If you think you are not feeling fresh and energetic even after six hours of sleep, try to sleep more.

2. Do Not Schedule Any Early Morning Meetings

Well, this is true. Set aside a couple of hours of the early morning for personal care and healthy family engagement. You might be wondering how this is related to productivity - yes, it has very direct relation to your success.

Jeff Bezos never schedules any early morning meetings as he personally loves to spend that time with his family and practicing some health improvement exercises. Also, Jeff Bezos believes that the thought of waking up very early just to attend a meeting is very stressful itself. If you go to bed at 10 p.m., you can enjoy an hour of extra restorative sleep and spend time with family in the morning. You do not have to rush. You can plan your day and do some physical exercises without taking any unnecessary stress.

3. Jeff Bezos Used to Keep Sleeping Bags Handy in His Office When Working On Wall Street

Yes, he is that serious about his sleep. When Jeff was working in computer science on Wall Street, he did not have the privilege of managing a sleeping schedule as per his convenience. But Jeff was smart and managed ways to address this problem. He used to bring a sleeping bag to work so that he could give his mind some extra energy boost when needed. He used to take frequent breaks and often used his breaks to take a power nap.

Jeff also recommends that people, who have no family waiting at home, should keep a sleeping bag handy at the office for those late night days. Is this not great?

This is how Jeff Bezos maintains his mental clarity and sharp thinking ability. It is important to note that you need to be very efficient in the prioritization of work so that you do not have to cut back on your sleep. You got few inspirational advices on prioritization from Warren Buffet. Now, let's see what else can be done to build a sharp mind and focus.

CHAPTER 6: HOW TO BE PRODUCTIVE THE STRESS-FREE WAYS?

LEARN FROM STEVE JOBS

Yes, it is true that our passion drives our energy and enthusiasm. We work hard to fulfill your dream and visions. Steve Jobs was renowned as a legendary visionary. However, despite his incredible success in Apple, Jobs was never known as a good leader to work with. He was often regarded as rude and a strict boss. Many of his ideas were confrontational.

But what was that thing that helped Steve Jobs keep his momentum of growth? He could dream and visualize the future a distinctive way. That is cool. But what is that one thing that helped him stay focused on his visions? Despite several challenges and interferences, how did he manage to work hard for his dream and meet his goals?

Here are a few things that Steve Job personally believed when he was alive:

1. Focus on What is Important, Declutter the Rest

You do not need to do a lot of things to be successful. Steve Jobs believes a person needs to work on the right things at the right time to be productive and successful. That is all. You cannot focus on a bunch of things at the same time. You cannot stand out that way. You have to choose what really matters and get rid of the rest.

2. Learn New Skills

Learn new skills to build a focused and productive mind. You do not have to excel at everything you learn, but you do that to put your mind into new challenges. This way your brain will be more creative.

3. Arrange Your Day Skilfully

You can arrange your day in a way that ensures working very productively. When you start a day, write down five or six things that you think you have been ignoring for long and must complete that day. Then review each of them and ask yourself, if you complete these tasks today, will it make a distinctive difference to your overall goal? Will it make you satisfied of your overall day utilization? Now, if you identify one or two of the overall 5 goals that are important, pick those ones and start working on them.

This is one of the most helpful habits that many other entrepreneurs, including Tim Ferris, follow in their day to day life. This is a practice of prioritization. Once you master the exercise, you will be able to overcome self-sabotaging habits that kill productivity easily.

Steve jobs also believe that one must delegate responsibilities to focus well on priorities. Do not attempt to do everything on your own.

So, according to Steve Jobs, these are the three most important rules for improving focus and productivity. These strategies worked for him. And these rules make sense as well, don't they?

Chapter 7: Reach Optimal Productivity a Different Way

Tony Robins inspires millions. But how does he inspire himself to remain productive every day of his life? Tony Robbins provided personal coaching to many well-known political figures. Each and every person has his/her own capacity of handling work burden. Some people can do a lot of work and manage a lot of stress without any problem, but, some people cannot.

During an interview with Business Insider, Tony Robins said he advises his clients to follow a technique call Rapid Planning Method (RPM). One thing you should know is that the productivity improvement ideas of Tony Robins slightly differ from the common belief.

You usually believe that you should start a day with a to-do list for task prioritization and organization. But Tony Robins does not believe in that concept. He says thinking that a to-do list can make a big difference in productivity is the biggest mistake. So here are some of his beliefs and thoughts on improving productivity:

23

1. Ask Yourself What You Want?

So how does it work? Break down your goal for your convenience. Do not think about what you want to achieve in a year. Instead, think what do you want to achieve in a month, week and then in a day. If you narrow down your goal, it will be easy for you to address the key aspects. So, first, think about what outcome you expect. You have to determine the objective of your actions. Why are you after your goals and objectives? Do not rush to make some to-do list without being sure about your ultimate objective. Making a to-do list will not serve your purpose if you are not clear about your dreams and visions.

2. Then Think Why Do You Want Them; Find Your Purpose

Tony Robins believe our intentions drive our actions. Your intentions have to be very strong to keep you focused on your goals. This is the reason you have to ask yourself why you want to achieve the goals you have set for yourself. Why do they matter so much? Find out the real driving force. When Tony Robins decided to work hard to be wealthy at a very young age, he did not take the thought of being rich as the real motivator. Instead, he visualized the happiness of being able to buy his mother a nice house, donating free meals to families and the scope of enjoying life as the powerful driving force.

3. Then Focus on Your Massive Action Plan

In the end, inspire yourself with a massive action plan. Tony Robins suggests every person should follow this process to approach his goals. This will efficiently cut down the obstacles that hamper progress and let a person focus strongly on his real goals.

Tony Robins recommend for wisdom improvisation. During the digital age, when we are buried under unlimited information, we are literally starving of wisdom. Try to make your wisdom stronger and intentions clear. Get a clear idea of what your purpose is and then work on it.

Experts have their own ways to make their days simple and productive. That's because every human being's skill, ability, talent, and priorities are different. Elon Musk is a very successful entrepreneur, we all know his story. He is busy, but still, he manages his time efficiently and has no complaints about that. Let's find out the secrets of his incredible productivity from his point of view.

CHAPTER 8: HOW CAN SOMEONE WORK FOR 100 HOURS A WEEK?

PRODUCTIVITY FROM ELON MUSK'S PERSPECTIVE

Elon Musk is almost a workaholic. He keeps his daily schedules tight and sticks to it. Where does he get his motivation? Yes, it is understandable that money drives motivation. But, Elon Musk has endured a lot of psychological abuse from his father and worked too hard to build his empire. It was never an easy journey for him, but he managed to survive all oddities and grow as a super power. What gave him so much strength? What kept him moving amid all challenges?

Like any ordinary man, Elon Musk had to work on his own weaknesses too. He worked very hard to overcome his fear, worries, and tensions. But, when most people tend to give up, he did not. Here are few things that Elon Musk likes to think to keep himself going and maintain his productivity:

1. He Takes Criticism Positively: Elon Musk does not fear to face criticism. This is one of the strategies that encourage him to seek ways for improvement. Of course, he also believes that criticism hurts and often times make him upset. But, the bright side of it is that gradually he gets over it and looks at the bigger picture. This actually gives him the courage to face his problems and solve them. So Elon Musk does not let criticisms become his distraction. He uses them to his advantage.

2. He Loves His Company As He Loves His Child: His love for his company is his biggest motivation for productivity. During several interviews, Elon Musk mentioned that building a company is like raising a child. He is so passionate about his work and company that any problem or challenge cannot discourage him. He does everything he can to make his company thrive. As many people know, he works almost 100 hours a week most of the times. This is crazy. No one can work that hard without the love and passion for work.

So yes, if you want to go by his rule, then you have to find love in your work. If you feel passionate about your work, productivity will automatically improve.

3. Elon Musk Can Multitask: Not everyone can do that. In fact, many life coaches and experts believe that multitasking ruins productivity, but Elon Mask does not identify himself with this common belief. He tries to combine several tasks together so that he can work on them simultaneously. He can check and answer emails while looking at a spreadsheet. Yes, he can do that and he does not feel overwhelmed. Musk also often uses his 30 minutes of lunch break to check his emails or for a meeting.

4. He Improves with Feedbacks: Musk loves to take feedbacks. He listens to constructive and honest feedbacks to improve. It helps him to focus on his goals better and keep his ideas fresh.

It is clear that Musk's motivation comes from his passion for work. He is exceptionally hardworking. No one can work that hard by force. It has to come from inside. So yes, Elon Musk's productivity secret might not fit in everybody's basket. Let's see what we can learn from other leaders famous for their superior productivity and success.

CHAPTER 9: PRODUCTIVITY IMPROVEMENT IS NOT A SECRET TECHNIQUE

LEARN HOW MARK CUBAN KEEPS HIMSELF SMART AND FOCUSED

You will be surprised to know that many entrepreneurs love to start their morning with their work. However, there is a reason they do that. Morning is the time when the mind is fresh. After enough hours of restorative sleep, the brain works at its peak during this time.

Different sources pointed at the fact that morning is the best time for indulging in a creative work. Especially, scientists say that the brain of the adults functions optimally in the morning as they gradually progress to aging. A brain engagement study conducted on 18 older participants closely observed their brain activities through FMRI. They found that all participants performed the given task efficiently in the morning between 8:30 a.m. and 10:30 a.m.

Why that happens is not clear. Several reasons can be associated. But that is what is true for Mark Cuban at least: He is a morning person; he thinks each day of his life should start with his business work, No better what start to a day is possible for him. This business magnet looks too much in love with his work, isn't it?

Well, this can be true for you as well. Some people find it easy to concentrate better in the early morning hours as there is always less disturbance and interference at those times. After all, we all need peace of mind to concentrate better. So how does Mark Cuban manage his time to work more efficiently?

1. Money Is not His Motivation, he Longs for Excellence

What inspires Mark Cuban is the desire to outperform. He works hard, but he does not work hard only to build his wealth. What drives his energy and enthusiasm is his desire to outwork and outlearn. He takes lessons from everything, even from his mistakes.

2. Mark Cuban is a Doer

He believes less in dreaming and more in doing. He knows how to act on his goals and spend less time thinking about it. Many people dream about their goals, but they fail to act on them. This is why not everyone is successful.

3. Practice Gratitude

Mark Cuban never takes his life for granted. He believes he is fortunate to have this life and opportunities. He works hard so that he can continue to perform well to retain what he has achieved. He recommends the same to others.

That's a nice gesture. We really appreciate his perspective. If you work with a mindset that if you do not work hard, someone else will take everything away from you, you will never take your work for granted. So, work productively to help your career and your life.

CHAPTER 10: HOW TO CRUSH YOUR WEAKNESS IF IT'S HOLDING YOU BACK

LEARN HOW ARNOLD USED HIS MIND TO BUILD HIS IRON STRONG BODY

Arnold's life and professional journey have been extremely interesting overall. Who knew a world class body builder would turn into a wonderful actor and then embark on a political career as a Governor of California? Arnold has played diversified roles as a successful athlete, actor, and politician. So what was the secret behind? What made him so versatile and an excellent performer in every sphere of life?

Like most successful people on earth, Arnold has also been seen to live life by a few simple rules. During different interviews with media, Arnold told them that he always tried to remain extremely disciplined throughout his life. A typical day of Arnold's life includes a lot of workouts, hard training, a huge amount of healthy diet, work, etc. But for productivity, Arnold likes to listen to his heart. Here are few things that Arnold recommends for success in life:

1. Trust Your Instinct: Arnold likes to listen to his heart and trust his instincts when it comes to work. He once said,

"We all have great inner power. The power is self-faith. There's really an attitude to winning. You have to see yourself winning before you win. And you have to be hungry. You have to want to conquer." (http://smartonlinesuccess.com/arnold-schwarzeneggers-six-rules-for-success/)

2. Try to Create or be in an Environment that Supports Good Habits: Developing new habits can be challenging. It will need a lot of mental strength and support. For example, if you want to start working early in the morning, but you are not a morning person, it is going to be a huge deal. Wouldn't it be nice if someone could help you wake up early morning and take you for running or jogging with him?

3. Start Making Small Steps and Celebrate the Victory: Habits do not change overnight. To work with concentration and a focused mind, you might have to follow few strategies. For example, working with frequent intervals, maintaining the same working schedule every day, developing new habits like reading to give the mind some refreshment time, etc. You will take the time to develop new habits that can keep your mental health well and improve your focus and attention. But for motivation, always make time to celebrate the small improvements.

4. Arnold Likes to Learn From the Stumbles: Many people quickly tend to give up when they fail, but in such case, Arnold acts with a different mindset. He does not get discouraged, he takes lessons from it and makes a new start.

CONCLUSION

This book has amazing facts on entrepreneur's and leader's productivity secrets. All these successful people turned their life with very distinctive approaches. Most of these people are not born genius. They are fighters and survivors. The only thing that makes these people different is that they do not know how to give up. They never stopped trying to improve despite the odd circumstances and failures.

Who was Tony Robins before he became a world-renowned public figure and icon? Despite his life situations, he knew from the beginning that he would turn his life into a major successful journey, which he did. He did not do it because he wanted to become famous, he did it because he wanted to make a change. He wanted to change his life and his circumstances and he knew what to do and how to do.

So you will also have to find out ways to change and improve. Take action today. Make a change.

ABOUT THE AUTHOR

Hi, I'm Paul and here's a little about me:

I'm an entrepreneur, internet marketer, author, life coach, professional speaker, fitness enthusiast, and world traveler. I feel extremely blessed for the life that I live.

I bring 7 years of niche expertise in self-help and personal development. I'm a business management graduate and I like to study people who appear to be unbeatable against all oddities or challenges of life. I seek answers for failures, lack of growth and thus I want to help people reinvent themselves. I believe: Each and every person is the sole controller of his/her life. If you do not take an utmost care of your life, no one else will.

More by Paul Goleman

PREVIEW OF: ANXIETY

HOW TO STOP WORRYING AND OVERCOME YOUR FEARS BY RELIEVING ANXIETY AND DEPRESSION, PANIC ATTACKS, SOCIAL ANXIETY AND STRESS

INTRODUCTION

Today's is a fast-paced, modern world where each day is filled with demands we must meet and deadlines we must make. We have a lot of commitments we must fulfill and a huge amount of responsibility that we undertake, especially in the professional fields, which, as the days go by, are becoming more and more competitive.

It isn't surprising, then, that a lot of people find themselves feeling quite anxious when they face a situation that could be potentially threatening to them. Stress comes in various forms to different people – a job interview for a newly graduated college student, a blind date for someone who doesn't date much, a deadline to meet with the really tough presentation to be given in front of the whole Board of Directors, etc. In these situations, it's normal to feel anxious, worried and even a little stressed out.

However, if your worries are constant, that is, they don't go away once the stressful situation has come to an end, or you're worrying about something that really doesn't warrant so much stress – there's a very big possibility that you're struggling with an anxiety disorder. This kind of stress interferes with the quality of your daily life and doesn't allow you to rest; it's the kind of stress and worry that cross the borders of daily concerns into the active fear that begins to overwhelm your everyday routine, and to the point whereby you cannot work and meet your commitments.

But hey! It isn't the end! Anxiety disorders come in different shapes and sizes, but they don't mean the end of your life, as you know it! Like any other physical disease, mental issues are also easily addressed – all you need is a little bit of patience and maturity to understand what you're dealing with and the different treatment options available. Once you know what you're afflicted with, you can easily take the necessary steps to regain control of your life.

In this book, we will investigate precisely what anxiety is, what the different types of anxiety are, and how you can get through having anxiety by employing both professional as well as self-help methods. We will look at some real-time, practical solutions you can practice on your own, to augment any professional help you might avail of!

CHAPTER 1: ANXIETY – AN OVERVIEW

As I said, an anxiety disorder is something that is not to be taken lightly. It can cause a number of issues and adversely affect the quality of life; it can also cause other physical health problems if not treated properly.

WHAT IS ANXIETY?

So before you can think about getting treatment for anxiety, first try to understand what anxiety is.

Anxiety, defined medically, is the body's natural response to danger; when you feel threatened by a situation, your body automatically responds with an adrenaline spike that leaves your heart thudding and your palms sweating. Now, this kind of fear, on a normal, day-to-day basis, under moderation, actually isn't a bad thing. Moderate anxiety can be helpful – it sharpens your senses, keeps you focused and motivates you to get things done.

However, when this anxiety translates itself into a debilitating panic or an overwhelming sense of fear of the things people wouldn't usually have issues facing – that's when things get bad. This kind of anxiety isn't a functional anxiety that is productive in any manner – it's a disorder that needs to be treated like any other physical disorder.

HOW TO IDENTIFY ANXIETY

An anxiety disorder is quite different from regular stress induced by a fast-paced life. That's not to say that such stress doesn't have adverse effects; just that an anxiety disorder is a much more pronounced problem – it's a magnified version of this stress that can cause disruption in your daily routine to the point of being, not just unproductive, but completely counterproductive!

Here are a few questions you can answer to identify if you're plagued with an anxiety disorder:

• How often are you tense, worried or afraid?

• Does this fear interfere with your ability to go about your day-to-day activities of work, school and the like?

• How often do you face fears that you know are irrational, but just can't seem to shake them?

• Do things have to be done in an exact, particular manner for you? Do you believe that you will fail or do you feel debilitating fear at the thought of it not being done on your own terms?

• Do you end up avoiding daily activities in your life – like going to a coffee shop with friends or walking out in public – because they cause you acute fear or worry?

• Do you have those sudden moments where your heart begins to race in utter panic and you have difficulty breathing?

• Do you feel like your life is spinning out of control and you'd like to stay in bed all day, simply because it's the only safe place you know without any kind of fear?

If the answers to all the questions given above are positive, then it is very much possible that you are suffering from an anxiety disorder. Remember, there are a number of disorders, each with their own specific problems, though they all overlap and in general, wreak havoc on your system. It's best to consult with a certified doctor before you attempt to treat yourself – you need to identify what type of anxiety you're suffering from before you can fix it.

SIGNS AND SYMPTOMS OF ANXIETY DISORDERS

The problem with anxiety is that it looks different on every person. Just as we all have our own unique and individual personalities, so too are our sets of triggers extremely different – where one person could have a random panic attack in the middle of a crowd, another could suffer from a debilitating fear of driving. Anxiety comes in different forms, shapes, and sizes – as with any mental disorder, it's customized to suit the individual.

Now, even though this problem makes it difficult to categorize anxiety and identify it, all anxiety disorders have one consistent characteristic – the existence and the persistence of a severe fear in a situation where a person without anxiety would not feel threatened.

These symptoms of anxiety are both emotional and physical. One major issue with most mental disorders, particularly anxiety, is that people tend to dismiss them as just being overly sensitive. The fact is – the person is not being sensitive; they're having a very real, human reaction to something that causes them pain. It's not different than stepping on a thorn and wanting to get rid of the pain in the foot, only that it's an invisible kind of pain that most people don't understand.

The emotional distress does translate itself into physical symptoms; the more emotionally distressed a person is, the worse the physical symptoms become. This is because your body is responding to the very real fear you're feeling – it's provoking your flight or fight response and you're stuck in a physiological state that can be terrifying if you don't understand what you're going through.

Take a quick look at the different types of symptoms you may experience in this following section…

TO CHECK OUT THE REST OF:

ANXIETY

HOW TO STOP WORRYING AND OVERCOME YOUR FEARS BY RELIEVING ANXIETY AND DEPRESSION, PANIC ATTACKS, SOCIAL ANXIETY AND STRESS

Search it on amazon as "Anxiety Paul Goleman"

Or go here for more books by Paul Goleman:

http://www.amazon.com/Paul-Goleman/e/B01EPDLLLO

ONE LAST THING...

If you enjoyed this book or found it useful I'd be very grateful if you'd post a short review on Amazon. Your support really does make a difference and I read all the reviews personally so I can get your feedback and make this book even better.

Thanks again for your support!

www.ingramcontent.com/pod-product-compliance
Lightning Source LLC
Chambersburg PA
CBHW070418190526
45169CB00003B/1315